make your first Quilt

with M'Liss Rae Hawley

Text copyright © 2007 by M'Liss Rae Hawley

Artwork copyright © 2007 by C&T Publishing, Inc.

Publisher: Amy Marson

Editorial Director: Gailen Runge

Acquisitions Editor: Jan Grigsby

Editor: Gailen Runge

Technical Editors: Gailen Runge, Majorie Russell, Carolyn Aune

Copyeditor/Proofreader: Wordfirm Inc.

Cover Designer: Kristy Zacharias

Book Designer: Kristen Yenche

Junior Designer: Kerry Graham

Illustrator: Gailen Runge

Production Coordinator: Tim Manibusan

Photography: Luke Mulks and Diane Pedersen, unless otherwise noted

Published by: C&T Publishing, Inc., P.O. Box 1456, Lafayette, CA 94549

Library of Congress Cataloging-in-Publication Data

Hawley, M'Liss Rae.

  Make your first quilt with M'Liss Rae Hawley : beginner's step-by-step guide, 9 fabulous blocks, tips
& techniques / M'Liss Rae Hawley.

     p. cm.

  Includes index.

  ISBN-13: 978-1-57120-466-0 (paper trade : alk. paper)

  ISBN-10: 1-57120-466-0 (paper trade : alk. paper)

  1. Quilting. 2. Patchwork. I. Title.

  TT835.H3485225 2007

  746.46'041--dc22

                          2007016122

Printed in China

10 9 8 7 6 5 4 3 2 1

Dedication

This book is dedicated to YOU, the beginning quilter. You are about to experience the joy, creativity, and community of the world of quilting. You will be part of and contribute to its rich legacy and continuingtraditions.

It's an honor to share my passion and love of quilting with you. *Enjoy!*

Acknowledgments

I would most gratefully like to thank the following people and companies that share my vision, enthusiasm, and love of quilting, both personally and professionally, for their contribution to the industry.

C&T Publishing: Amy Marson, Jan Grigsby, Darra Williamson, Gailen Runge, Kerry Graham, Tim Manibusan, and all the staff who continue to create wonderful books.

Electric Quilt

Husqvarna Viking

Jo-Ann Fabrics and Crafts Store

Quilters Dream Batting

Robison-Anton Textiles

Sulky of America

Peggy Johnson, the Keeper of the Blocks, who helped draft the blocks in the book with The Electric Quilt Company software.

And thank you to my friends **Vicki DeGraaf, Peggy Johnson, Susie Kincy,** and **John James,** for helping with piecing and bindings!

Finally, thank you to **Michael,**

Adrienne,

and **Alexander**—my family.

Contents

Introduction

You are about to set off on an exciting journey of color, fabric, design, and stitching that will bring a whole new dimension of creativity into your life. Welcome to the world of quilting!

About 20 years ago, when I first started to teach quilting, I began with a Block-of-the-Month sampler quilt. (A visitor to my home will still see sampler blocks used as a border in our family room. It's constantly being updated and I also have a Christmas version.) For this sampler project I chose each block with care, so that each would build upon skills learned in the previous lessons, while also offering a new skill or technique to develop. I believed then, as I still believe these many years later, that the sampler quilt is a natural way to introduce a newcomer to quilting.

The sampler quilt you'll be making was created especially for this book, using today's fabrics and today's updated tools and methods. Many of the blocks, however, are the same classics, such as Waterwheel (page 32) and Ohio Star (page 43), that I included in that class so many years ago. I've teamed these classics with a few new favorites that I designed, such as Spinning My Wheels (page 34) and Useless Bay (page 36), to give the quilt a fresh, up-to-the-minute feeling.

Everything you need to guide you through the process of making your very first quilt is here. My hope is that you will carry this little book with you to the quilt shop or fabric store when you purchase your supplies and will keep it open by your sewing machine as you follow the step-by-step, illustrated instructions. This book was designed to help you choose the right tools, master and build skills, develop confidence, and achieve accurate results, all of which add up to a successful and joyful quilting experience. I've even included instructions for constructing a simple pillow or two out of your favorite blocks. Use these little pillows to complete the ensemble or give them as gifts to family and friends.

Enjoy the experience!

Getting Ready

As with any first-time venture, it is important that you recognize and understand the key components of your new undertaking. It is also important that you assemble the best tools and materials for the job. You'll find lots of help in the next few pages!

binding   outer border   block   inner border

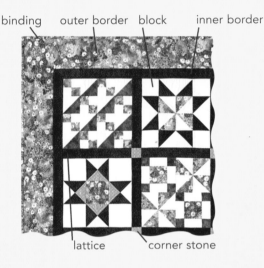

lattice   corner stone

Anatomy of a Quilt

A **quilt** is basically a three-layer fabric "sandwich." A **sampler quilt**—the kind of quilt you will be making—is composed of a series of different blocks. When these blocks are sewn together and borders are added, the result is called the **quilt top**.

The finished quilt top is layered with filler—called **batting**—and a **backing** fabric, and the three layers are then secured together with stitching. This stitching may be decorative or strictly utilitarian; in either case, it is called **quilting.** Finally, the edges of the stitched quilt sandwich are finished with fabric strips, called **binding**.

Here are some additional terms you'll be hearing again and again as you read through these pages and construct your very first quilt:

A **block** is a section of the quilt that forms a self-contained design. Some designs are literal, such as stars or pinwheels. Others are more abstract. A block is usually square, but it may also be rectangular or any other geometric shape.

All the blocks in this sampler are pieced blocks. Pieced blocks are made up of **units**, or smaller squares and rectangles that are sewn together to make the design. Units may be squares or rectangles cut from a single piece of fabric, or they may themselves be pieced from smaller squares, rectangles, or even triangles. More on that later!

The blocks in this sampler quilt are separated by **lattice strips**. (You may sometimes see these strips referred to as **sashing**.) Lattice strips are especially effective in sampler quilts; they act as a frame to highlight each block.

Cornerstones are little squares that appear at the corners of the blocks where the vertical and horizontal lattice strips meet. While they are not essential—the vertical or horizontal lattice can be cut from a single long strip—these squares make a lovely design element and sometimes even create secondary designs with the corners of adjacent blocks.

Many quilts have **borders** that surround the quilt top on all four sides, much like a frame surrounds a painting. This quilt is no exception: it has a narrow **inner border** (think of a mat in a picture frame) and a wider **outer border** that completes the overall design. These borders are typically made from fabrics already in the quilt top.

Sewing Machine and Other Tools

You don't need a lot of fancy gadgets or special equipment to make a quilt. Here is a list of what you'll need, with thoughts about my favorite features.

Sewing Machine

First of all, you'll need a **sewing machine**. It doesn't need to be the very latest model, with all the bells and whistles, but it should be in good working order, with a dependable straight stitch. Outfit it with a new needle before you begin this or any project. If it's been awhile since your machine has been serviced, bring it to a shop and get a tune-up. It will make your sewing experience much smoother.

A **dual-feed foot** (also called a walking foot) is a must for straight-line machine quilting and is also useful for applying binding by machine. An **open-toe stippling foot** (also called a darning foot) is useful for free-motion machine quilting. These two attachments are pictured on page 54.

Tools and Notions

You'll find the following tools and notions at your local quilt shop or home sewing store.

Rotary cutter: This cutting tool, similar to a pizza cutter, makes cutting fabric strips and pieces a breeze. Look for one with an ergonomic grip and a reliable safety catch. The blade does eventually become dull, so it's a good idea to keep a package of replacement blades on hand.

Cutting mat: This special cutting surface can stand up to a sharp rotary blade without sustaining damage. It comes in a variety of sizes; 18″ × 24″ is a good, versatile size for your first purchase. I like the green, gridded variety. Lines indicating 45° angles are also helpful.

Acrylic rulers: You'll come to love these sturdy rulers, which typically include all the measurements and increments essential to the new quilter. Try the 6″ × 24″ and 6″ × 12″ sizes, preferably with 45° angles indicated.

Ruler grips: These clear, adhesive tabs stick to the bottom of your acrylic rulers to keep them from slipping as you cut.

Pins: My favorites are fine, glass-head silk pins, because they don't leave unsightly holes in the fabric.

Scissors: You'll need both fabric scissors and small embroidery-type scissors for cutting thread.

Seam ripper: Even the most experienced quilter makes a mistake now and then! This tool allows you to cut the stitches in a misplaced seam easily. These tools come with an ergonomic handle as well.

Thread: Select 100% cotton thread in a neutral color for piecing—both on top and in the bobbin. Hand quilters can use 100% cotton or cotton-coated polyester hand-quilting thread in the color of their choice. Cotton, rayon, polyester, monofilament, or any number of specialty threads designed for machine quilting are also available to the machine quilter.

Batting: You will need a piece of batting approximately $62\frac{1}{2}″ \times 62\frac{1}{2}″$ for your quilt. See page 50 for suggestions on what to look for.

Choosing and Preparing Fabric

Many quilters agree: Selecting the fabric is one of the most exciting parts of making a quilt. It can also be the most overwhelming, especially for a beginner—there are just so many wonderful choices out there! Here are some suggestions for an enjoyable—and successful—fabric experience.

Because I am a purist, I prefer to use 100% cotton fabrics in my quilts. I recommend that you do, too! Cotton is soft, easy to work with, wears well, and is very forgiving. In general, I strongly suggest that you stay away from polyester and cotton-polyester blends, which have a tendency to ravel and can be slippery and difficult to handle.

Prewashing your fabrics, a practice I advocate, will preshrink the fabric, remove any excess finishing chemicals, and make the fabric softer to the touch. I prewash all new fabric—small pieces in the sink, and ½ yard and larger pieces in the washing machine. Next comes the ironing: straight from the dryer, you can iron fabrics, square them up (page XX), and put them on the shelf in no time.

Understanding Your Fabric

Cotton fabric is woven so it has a lengthwise and crosswise direction.

It helps to understand this so you can best determine how to cut your fabrics for piecing.

The fabric is finished with a tightly woven edge along the two lengthwise sides. This is called the **selvage**. Because selvages are more tightly woven, you will need to trim them off before using the fabric.

The **lengthwise** direction (or lengthwise grain) runs parallel to the selvage. The lengthwise grain has little, if any, give.

The **crosswise** direction (or crosswise grain) runs across the width of the fabric, from selvage to selvage. This grain has a slight bit of give.

Any angle that does not run precisely **parallel** or perpendicular to the selvage—that is, one that runs on the diagonal of the fabric—is called the **bias** of the fabric. The bias has lots of stretch, so you will want to avoid having this stretchy edge fall on the outside edge of a unit or block.

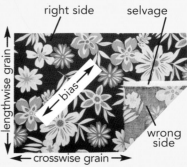

right side   selvage

lengthwise grain

bias

wrong side

← crosswise grain →

What—and How Much—to Buy

You will need five different fabrics (Fabrics A–E) to create the quilt top for your sampler quilt. How do you decide—from the loads of options available—which to choose?

The main thing that you'll want your five fabrics to have is contrast. Without contrast between the fabrics, the design, no matter how perfectly pieced, will disappear in the finished quilt.

You can create contrast by taking advantage of three key elements:

Color • Value • Fabric Print

You deal with color every day, so I won't bother explaining that one! However, value and fabric print may be new terms to you. **Value** simply refers to how light or dark a fabric appears when placed next to its neighbors. **Fabric print** refers to what design or motif appears on the fabric—a stripe, a flower, a polka dot, and so on.

I often encourage students, especially first-time quilters, to begin by choosing a multicolor fabric with a medium- to large-scale print that they absolutely *love* and then to use that fabric as the basis for choosing the quilt's other, "supporting" fabrics. You might choose a particular **theme fabric**—called a focus fabric by some—

Fabric Grain Guide

You have found the perfect coordinating fabric to match your project, but the selvage has been removed. What do you do? There's an easy way to find your fabric's grainline: Place your left hand along one of the fabric edges. Next, place your other hand about six inches away from the first hand along the same edge. Now give the fabric a sharp tug. If the fabric "snaps," you're holding the lengthwise grain. If it makes a dull "thud," you're holding the crosswise grain.

because it includes your favorite colors or because it depicts a holiday or special memory.

Here are the fabrics you'll need for your quilt. All yardages are based on fabric that is approximately 42″–44″ wide on the bolt and assume a usable width of 40″ after the fabric has been laundered and prepared for cutting.

The swatches illustrate the fabrics I selected for my sampler quilt (page 23 and in detail throughout). Notice the contrast in color, value, and fabric print among my five choices. I encourage you to use my choices as a guide only; pick your fabrics in the colors and theme that appeal to you.

FABRIC A *(Background Fabric)*

This fabric should be the lightest fabric of the five so you are sure to get lots of value contrast with the other fabrics.

You will need **1½ yards** of Fabric A to use as the background for each block, with the exception of Block 1: Triple Rail, where this fabric will play a supporting role.

I chose a crisp white-on-white print.

FABRIC B *(Theme Fabric)*

This is the fabric that sets the color scheme and tone for your entire quilt.

You will need **2⅜ yards** of Fabric B to use for the outer border and binding, as well as in every block.

I selected a large-scale floral print in predominantly reds (including pinks), violets, blues, and greens, with touches of white for sparkle.

FABRIC C *(Supporting Fabric)*

Use your theme fabric to select a strong supporting player—perhaps one of the brighter colors in your theme fabric.

You will need **½ yard** of Fabric C for Blocks 1: Triple Rail, 2: Log Cabin, 5: Spinning My Wheels, 6: Useless Bay, and 7: Jewel Box.

I chose a deep, rich, tone-on-tone red fabric.

FABRIC D *(Contrasting Fabric)*

Since it will be used for the lattice to frame the blocks, a fabric with lots of contrast in value to your background fabric (Fabric A), but without too much print, works well here.

You will need 1 1/4 **yards** of Fabric D for the lattice and inner border of your quilt and for Blocks 2: Log Cabin, 3: Churn Dash, 4: Waterwheel, 8: Tumbling Star, and 9: Ohio Star.

My choice was a dark violet in a subtle, tone-on-tone, dotted print.

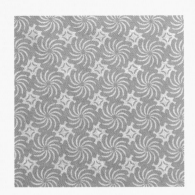

FABRIC E *(Medium-Value Fabric)*

A medium-value fabric, in a medium-scale print is a good choice for Fabric E.

You will need 1/2 **yard** of Fabric E for the lattice cornerstones, as well as for blocks 3: Churn Dash, 7: Jewel Box, and 9: Ohio Star.

I used a medium-value green in a regularly repeating print that added a linear touch to my otherwise "organic" fabric selections.

BACKING FABRIC

This can be any good-quality cotton fabric you like: one of the fabrics you've used on the quilt top or another fabric complementary in color and/or print. Just be sure it is not so dark that it will show through to the lightest fabrics on the front of the quilt.

You will need 3 1/2 **yards** of fabric for the back of your quilt.

I used the theme fabric.

Using a Color Tool

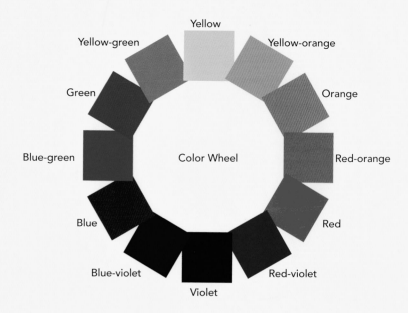

The color wheel was designed to illustrate the 12 pure colors—the three primary colors (red, yellow, and blue), the three secondary colors (orange, green, and violet), and the six tertiary or intermediary colors (yellow-orange, red-orange, red-violet, blue-violet, blue-green, and yellow-green)—and the relationships among them. I often use the color wheel as an additional guideline for choosing the color schemes for my quilts.

Here are a few color schemes you can select based on the color wheel:

A **monochromatic** color scheme is based on a single color in all its various tints, tones, and shades.

Monochromatic color scheme

A **complementary** color scheme pairs colors that appear directly across from each other on the color wheel—for example, red and green, blue and orange, and yellow and purple. Each color is balanced by its opposite (or complementary) color.

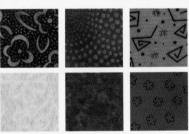

Complementary color schemes

A **split complementary** scheme is a three-color scheme created by combining a single color with the two colors beside its complement—for example, yellow, red-violet, and blue-violet (the latter being the colors on either side of violet, yellow's complement).

Split complementary color scheme

An **analogous** color scheme is made up of colors that appear side by side on the color wheel—for example,

red, red-orange, and orange. Quilts based on this color scheme work because the three or four colors have an element of color in common with their neighbors.

Analogous color scheme

Cutting and Piecing

This chapter includes the nuts and bolts of cutting, pinning, assembling, and pressing the pieces, units, and blocks in your quilt.

Rotary Cutting Strips and Pieces

All pieces for the quilt and the pillows in this book can be cut with a rotary cutter. It is essential that you square the edges of your fabrics before you rotary cut them into strips and pieces. The edges of the fabric must be straight for the resulting pieces to be straight, and you don't want to waste time—or precious fabric!—by having to stop and recut. I recommend pre-washing your fabrics. Make sure the fabric is pressed and that you fold it carefully before you begin cutting. If you have a large piece of yardage, fold it twice or cut it into shorter lengths so that you can work with a more manageable amount.

Note: Cutting instructions are for right-handers. Reverse if you are left-handed.

To Square Up Your Fabric

1. Place the folded fabric on the cutting mat with the folded edge facing you. Position your ruler on the right edge of the fabric so it is perpendicular to the fold.

2. Trim a narrow strip from the edge of the fabric to square it up. Rotate the fabric (or the mat) and repeat to trim the opposite edge.

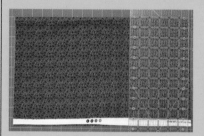

Cutting Strips, Squares, and Rectangles

Use your ruler to measure and cut strips and pieces. Use the grid on the mat for aligning the fabric and for taking general measurements, not for making precise measurements.

1. Working from the squared left edge of the fabric, use the lines in your acrylic ruler to measure and cut a strip of the desired width. Repeat to cut the required number of strips. You may need to square up the end after every few cuts. (Note: The width of your first cut is always listed first.)

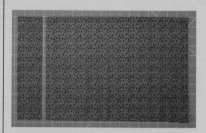

2. Cut the strips into squares or rectangles, as directed in the project instructions.

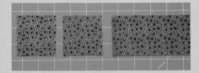

Cutting Triangles

Some of the blocks in the quilt contain quarter-square triangles and half-square triangles. Although the triangles look the same and both start with squares, there is one key difference: In a half-square triangle, the straight grain (lengthwise and crosswise) falls on the two short sides of the shape, and the long diagonal edge falls on the stretchy bias. With a quarter-square triangle, the long diagonal edge falls on the straight grain (lengthwise or crosswise), while the stretchy bias falls on the two short sides.

Quarter-square triangle   *Half-square triangle*

Whether you cut half- or quarter-square triangles will depend on where you want the straight grain of the triangle to fall in the unit or block. In most cases, this will be on the outside edge.

In either case, begin by cutting squares as described in Cutting Strips, Squares, and Rectangles (page 16).

To make half-square triangles, use your rotary cutter and ruler to divide each square from corner to corner in one direction, as shown. Each square yields two half-square triangles with the straight of grain (lengthwise and crosswise) on the two short sides.

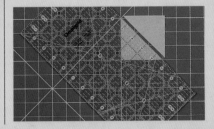

Here's a quick
solution that
will adapt
your machine
for precise
piecing if your
presser foot

¼″
does not measure an exact
¼″ seam. Place your acrylic
rotary-cutting ruler under the
needle, lower the presser
foot, and drop the needle so
it lands exactly on the ruler's
¼″ marking. Place a piece of
masking tape (or drafting
tape for a more temporary
solution) on the throat plate
of the machine, right along
the edge of the ruler. This
will be your guide for lining
up the raw edges of your
fabric pieces to sew a
perfect seam!

To make quarter-square triangles, use
your rotary cutter and ruler to divide
each square from corner to corner in
both directions, as shown. Each square
yields four quarter-square triangles
with the straight of grain (lengthwise
or crosswise) on the long diagonal side.

Piecing and Pressing

Quilters use a ¼″ **seam allowance**
for piecing units and blocks and
for assembling quilt tops. All cut
measurements shown in this book
include a ¼″ seam allowance.

Sewing an accurate ¼″ seam is
essential if you want the pieces, units,
blocks, and borders of your quilt top
to fit together. It's always a good idea
to check that *your* ¼″ seam is accurate before beginning to sew.

Testing Your Seam Allowance

Cut two strips of scrap fabric, each
1½″ × 3½″. With right sides together,
sew the strips together along one
3½″ side. Carefully press in the
direction shown by the arrows and
measure the finished unit. It should
measure exactly 2½″ wide. If it does
not, try again until you are able to
sew a perfect ¼″ seam.

Assembling the Blocks

You'll sew pieces into units and units
into rows. You'll then sew the rows
together to complete each block.
I'll tell you which way to press the
seams, either in the
instructions themselves or
with arrows in the accom-
panying diagrams.
Typically you will press
toward the darker
fabric or in the opposite

2½″

direction from the adjacent units so the seams "nest" nicely when you match and pin them for sewing.

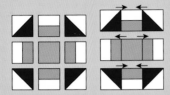

Note: In most cases, piecing diagrams show finished units and blocks; that is, without the seam allowances.

Unit with seam allowances   Finished unit

For perfect block assembly, follow these tips:

- Place all pieces, units, and rows right sides together for assembly.

- Align raw edges as described in the project instructions.

- Use those pins! When joining units into rows and joining rows together, pin to match seams and ends first, then add extra pins as needed.

- If one piece, unit, or row is larger than the other, pin as usual and then sew with the larger piece on the bottom and against the throat

plate of the machine. The action of the feed dogs will help ease the larger piece to fit.

- Press each seam as you sew it. Press lightly with a lifting-and-lowering motion. Dragging the iron across the fabric can distort the individual pieces and finished blocks.

Time-Savers

You'll love these fast and easy techniques. They not only save time, but help you improve your accuracy as well.

Starter scraps are little pieces of fabric, scraps, that when used at the beginning of your piecing will prevent your machine from gobbling the little triangle corners of your fabric. It works both on single pieces and in chain piecing. Begin your stitching on a small starter scrap before feeding onto the real thing. Works every time!

Chain Piecing

This technique saves time and thread when you need to stitch a series of identical pieces or units together. Simply feed and stitch the units one after another, without lifting the presser foot or cutting the thread in between. When you are finished, remove the "chain" from the machine and clip the threads in between to separate them.

Chain piecing

Strip Piecing

This technique comes in handy when you need to sew squares and/or rectangles together to make multiple, identical units, such as the four-patch units in blocks such as Block 6: Useless Bay (page 36) and Block 7: Jewel Box (page 38). Instead of sewing individual pieces together over and over, you sew strips together to make strip sets, or strata; "slice" or crosscut the sets into segments; and then rearrange and sew the segments together to complete the unit.

1. With right sides together, sew the strips together along their long edges in the order given in the project instructions. Press the seams as shown in the accompanying diagrams.

2. Use your rotary cutter and ruler to cut segments from the strip set in the width given in the project instructions.

3. Proceed to arrange and assemble the segments as described in the project instructions.

Sew and Flip

You'll love this quick-and-easy piecing method! Using only squares and rectangles, you'll achieve perfect little triangles on such blocks as Block 7: Jewel Box (page 38) and Block 8: Tumbling Star (page 41).

1. Use a ruler and marking tool to draw a diagonal line from corner to corner on the wrong side of each small square, as indicated in the directions for the block you are making.

2. With raw edges aligned, place the small marked square right sides together with the larger square or rectangle, as indicated in the block directions. Sew directly on the diagonal line.

3. Cut away the excess fabric, leaving a ¼″ seam allowance. Press the seams toward the small square.

4. Repeat Steps 2 and 3 to add additional squares, as needed.

Shopping List

- [ ] Sewing machine
  - sewing machine needles
  - $1/4$"-wide foot (for piecing)
  - dual-feed foot (for quilting; optional)
  - open-toe stippling foot (for quilting; optional)
- [ ] Rotary cutter
  - extra blade for cutter
- [ ] Cutting mat
- [ ] Acrylic rulers
  - ruler grips
- [ ] Pins
- [ ] Fabric scissors
- [ ] Small embroidery scissors
- [ ] Seam ripper
- [ ] Color wheel/color tool
- [ ] Iron
- [ ] Quilting stencils and/or patterns (optional)
- [ ] Marking tool (e.g., chalk; water-soluble marker)

- [ ] Long needle (for basting)
- [ ] Masking tape
- [ ] Hoop or frame (for hand quilting; optional)
- [ ] Hand-quilting needles (betweens; optional)
- [ ] Neutral 100% cotton thread (for piecing and machine quilting)
- [ ] Decorative thread (for quilting; optional)
- [ ] Quilting thread (for hand quilting; optional)
- [ ] Fabric
  - Fabric A (background fabric): $1\frac{1}{2}$ yards
  - Fabric B (theme fabric for blocks, outer border, binding): $2\frac{3}{8}$ yards
  - Fabric C (blocks): $\frac{1}{2}$ yard
  - Fabric D (blocks, lattice, inner border): $1\frac{1}{4}$ yards
  - Fabric E (blocks, cornerstones): $\frac{1}{2}$ yard
- [ ] Backing: $3\frac{1}{2}$ yards
- [ ] Batting ($62\frac{1}{2}$" $\times$ $62\frac{1}{2}$")

Making the Blocks

Now that you've gathered your tools, selected and prepared your fabric, and read about using a rotary cutter, piecing, and pressing your blocks, you are ready to begin stitching your first quilt. Here are a few reminders to keep in mind as you work.

Each finished block measures 12″ × 12″. Your unfinished blocks should measure 12½″ × 12½″ (see Squaring the Blocks, page 45). The completed quilt measures 54½″ × 54½″.

Checklist

- Read through the instructions for each block before you begin to cut and sew.

- To remove wrinkles and creases, press all fabrics before cutting them.

- Cut pieces in the order shown.

- Keep the rotary-cutter blade closed when you are not using it.

- Test all fabric markers on the fabrics you are using to be certain you can remove the markings later.

- Test your sewing machine for a perfect $\frac{1}{4}''$ seam allowance (page 18). Adjust as necessary.

- Pin pieces and units together with right sides together and raw edges aligned, carefully matching seams (page 19).

- Press seam allowances as you go in the direction indicated by the arrows in the diagrams.

- Measure each unit as you go.

- Carefully press the finished block.

Note: When you cut squares for a block, cut a strip the width of the square across the entire fabric (40″). Cut your squares and save the rest of the strip for use in other blocks. For example, you need to cut 4 squares $3\frac{1}{2}'' \times 3\frac{1}{2}''$ for Block 7: Jewel Box. Cut a strip $3\frac{1}{2}''$ wide. Cut the 4 squares. Use the rest of the strip when you cut the 4 squares $3\frac{1}{2}'' \times 3\frac{1}{2}''$ for Block 8: Tumbling Star.

First Things First: Cutting the Lattice and Border

The lattice and border strips are often the largest pieces you will cut for your quilt top, so it is a good idea to cut them first so you have enough fabric to cut the strips intact. You can cut the binding strips now, too. Cut all strips from the crosswise grain of the fabric (from selvage to selvage). Label them (outer border, inner border, and so on) and set them aside until you are ready to use them.

FROM FABRIC B:

Cut 5 strips, 6″ × 40″, for the outer border.

Cut 6 strips, 3″ × 40″, for the binding.

FROM FABRIC D:

Cut 5 strips, $2\frac{1}{4}'' \times 40''$, for the inner border.

Cut 4 strips, $2\frac{1}{4}'' \times 40''$; crosscut 12 strips, $2\frac{1}{4}'' \times 12\frac{1}{2}''$, for the lattice.

FROM FABRIC E:

Cut 4 squares, $2\frac{1}{4}'' \times 2\frac{1}{4}''$, for the lattice cornerstones.

Triple Rail

Cutting

Cut all strips from the crosswise grain of the fabric (from selvage to selvage).

   FABRICS A–C:
Cut 2 strips, 1½″ × 40″.

Assembling the Block

This block uses the Strip Piecing technique (page 20).

1. Arrange a Fabric A strip, a Fabric B strip, and a Fabric C strip as shown.

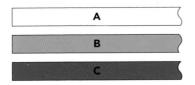

Sew the Fabric A strip and the Fabric B strip right sides together along one long edge. Press.

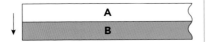

Repeat to sew the Fabric C strip to the opposite long edge of the Fabric

B strip. Press. Make 2 A/B/C strip sets. Each strip set should measure 3½″ × 40″.

Make 2 strip sets.

2. Cut a total of 16 segments, each 3½″ wide, from the strip sets you made in Step 1.

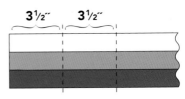

3½″   3½″

Cut 16 segments.

3. Arrange 4 units from Step 2, taking care to rotate them as shown.

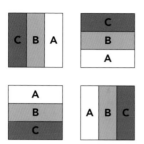

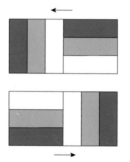

Sew the units together in pairs. Press.

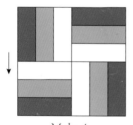

Sew the pairs together, carefully matching the center seam. Press. Make 4. Each unit should measure $6\frac{1}{2}'' \times 6\frac{1}{2}''$.

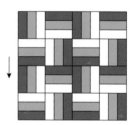

Make 4.

4. Arrange the 4 units from Step 3 as shown.

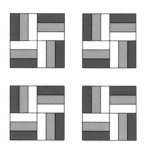

Sew the units together in pairs. Press.

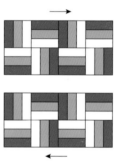

Sew the pairs together. Press. The block should measure $12\frac{1}{2}'' \times 12\frac{1}{2}''$.

Log Cabin

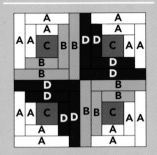

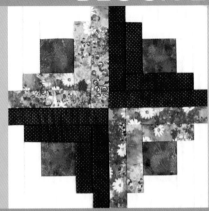

Cutting

Cut all strips from the crosswise grain of the fabric (from selvage to selvage).

FROM FABRIC C:

Cut 4 squares, $2\frac{1}{2}'' \times 2\frac{1}{2}''$.

FROM FABRIC A:

Cut 2 strips, $1\frac{1}{2}'' \times 40''$; crosscut:

4 pieces, $1\frac{1}{2}'' \times 2\frac{1}{2}''$;   4 pieces, $1\frac{1}{2}'' \times 3\frac{1}{2}''$;

4 pieces, $1\frac{1}{2}'' \times 4\frac{1}{2}''$;   4 pieces, $1\frac{1}{2}'' \times 5\frac{1}{2}''$.

FROM FABRIC B:

Cut 1 strip, $1\frac{1}{2}'' \times 40''$; crosscut:

2 pieces, $1\frac{1}{2}'' \times 3\frac{1}{2}''$;   2 pieces, $1\frac{1}{2}'' \times 4\frac{1}{2}''$;

2 pieces, $1\frac{1}{2}'' \times 5\frac{1}{2}''$;   2 pieces, $1\frac{1}{2}'' \times 6\frac{1}{2}''$.

FROM FABRIC D:

Cut 1 strip, $1\frac{1}{2}'' \times 40''$; crosscut:

2 pieces, $1\frac{1}{2}'' \times 3\frac{1}{2}''$;   2 pieces, $1\frac{1}{2}'' \times 4\frac{1}{2}''$;

2 pieces, $1\frac{1}{2}'' \times 5\frac{1}{2}''$;   2 pieces, $1\frac{1}{2}'' \times 6\frac{1}{2}''$.

Assembling the Block

1. Sew a $1\frac{1}{2}'' \times 2\frac{1}{2}''$ Fabric A piece to a $2\frac{1}{2}'' \times 2\frac{1}{2}''$ Fabric C square. Press. Working counterclockwise, repeat to sew a $1\frac{1}{2}'' \times 3\frac{1}{2}''$ Fabric A piece to the adjacent side of the unit. Press. Make 2.

Make 2.

2. Continuing to work counterclockwise, sew a $1\frac{1}{2}'' \times 3\frac{1}{2}''$ Fabric B piece to the next adjacent side of each unit from Step 1. Press. Sew a $1\frac{1}{2}'' \times 4\frac{1}{2}''$ Fabric B piece to the remaining side of the unit. Press. Make 2. Each unit should measure $4\frac{1}{2}'' \times 4\frac{1}{2}''$.

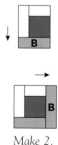

Make 2.

3. Beginning on the same side of the unit as you did in Step 1, sew a $1\frac{1}{2}'' \times 4\frac{1}{2}''$ Fabric A piece to the unit from Step 2. Press. Working counterclockwise, repeat to sew a $1\frac{1}{2}'' \times 5\frac{1}{2}''$ Fabric A piece to the adjacent side of the unit. Press. Make 2.

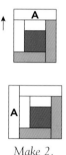

Make 2.

4. Continuing to work counterclockwise, sew a $1\frac{1}{2}'' \times 5\frac{1}{2}''$ Fabric B piece to the next adjacent side of each unit from Step 1. Press. Sew a $1\frac{1}{2}'' \times 6\frac{1}{2}''$ Fabric B piece to the remaining side of the unit. Press. Make 2. Each unit should measure $6\frac{1}{2}'' \times 6\frac{1}{2}''$.

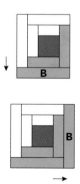

Make 2.

5. Repeat Steps 1–4 to make 2 additional units, this time substituting the $1\frac{1}{2}" \times 3\frac{1}{2}"$, $1\frac{1}{2}" \times 4\frac{1}{2}"$, $1\frac{1}{2}" \times 5\frac{1}{2}"$, and $1\frac{1}{2}" \times 6\frac{1}{2}"$ Fabric D strips for the corresponding Fabric B strips. Press. Make 2. Each unit should measure $6\frac{1}{2}" \times 6\frac{1}{2}"$.

Make 2.

6. Arrange the 2 units from Step 4 and the 2 units from Step 5, taking care to position and rotate them as shown.

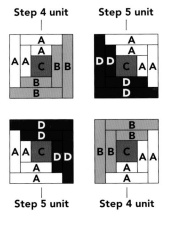

Sew the units together in pairs. Press.

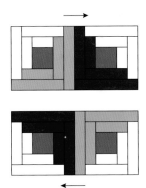

Sew the pairs together, carefully matching the center seam. Press. The block should measure $12\frac{1}{2}" \times 12\frac{1}{2}"$.

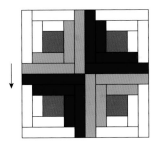

BLOCK 3

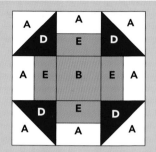

Cutting

Cut all strips from the crosswise grain of the fabric (from selvage to selvage).

 FROM FABRIC A:

Cut 1 strip, $2\frac{1}{2}'' \times 40''$; crosscut 4 pieces, $2\frac{1}{2}'' \times 4\frac{1}{2}''$.

Cut 2 squares, $4\frac{7}{8}'' \times 4\frac{7}{8}''$; cut each square once diagonally to make 2 half-square triangles (4 total).

 FROM FABRIC B:

Cut 1 square, $4\frac{1}{2}'' \times 4\frac{1}{2}''$.

 FROM FABRIC D:

Cut 2 squares, $4\frac{7}{8}'' \times 4\frac{7}{8}''$; cut each square once diagonally to make 2 half-square triangles (4 total).

 FROM FABRIC E:

Cut 1 strip, $2\frac{1}{2}'' \times 40''$; crosscut 4 pieces, $2\frac{1}{2}'' \times 4\frac{1}{2}''$.

Assembling the Block

1. Sew a Fabric A half-square triangle and a Fabric D half-square triangle together. Press. Make 4. Each unit should measure $4\frac{1}{2}'' \times 4\frac{1}{2}''$.

Make 4.

2. Sew a $2\frac{1}{2}'' \times 4\frac{1}{2}''$ Fabric A piece to a $2\frac{1}{2}'' \times 4\frac{1}{2}''$ Fabric E piece. Press. Make 4. Each unit should measure $4\frac{1}{2}'' \times 4\frac{1}{2}''$.

Make 4.

3. Arrange the 4 units from Step 1, the 4 units from Step 2, and the $4\frac{1}{2}'' \times 4\frac{1}{2}''$ Fabric B square.

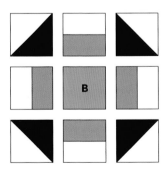

Sew the units and square together into rows. Press.

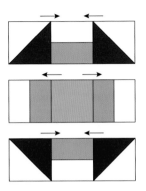

Sew the rows together, carefully matching the seams. Press. The block should measure $12\frac{1}{2}'' \times 12\frac{1}{2}''$.

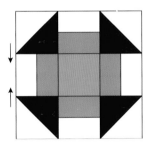

BLOCK 4

Waterwheel

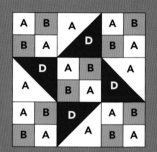

Cutting

Cut all strips from the crosswise grain of the fabric (from selvage to selvage).

FROM FABRIC A:
Cut 2 squares, $4\frac{7}{8}'' \times 4\frac{7}{8}''$; cut each square once diagonally to make 2 half-square triangles (4 total).

Cut 1 strip, $2\frac{1}{2}'' \times 40''$.

FROM FABRIC B:
Cut 1 strip, $2\frac{1}{2}'' \times 40''$.

FROM FABRIC D:
Cut 2 squares, $4\frac{7}{8}'' \times 4\frac{7}{8}''$; cut each square once diagonally to make 2 half-square triangles (4 total).

Assembling the Block

This block uses the Strip Piecing technique (page 20).

1. Sew a Fabric A half-square triangle and a Fabric D half-square triangle together. Press. Make 4. Each unit should measure $4\frac{1}{2}'' \times 4\frac{1}{2}''$.

Make 4.

2. Arrange the $2\frac{1}{2}'' \times 40''$ Fabric A strip and the $2\frac{1}{2}'' \times 40''$ Fabric B strip as shown.

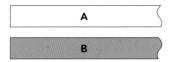

Sew the Fabric A strip and the Fabric B strip right sides together along a long edge. Press. The strip set should measure $4\frac{1}{2}'' \times 40''$.

3. Cut a total of 10 segments, each $2\frac{1}{2}''$ wide, from the strip set in Step 2.

2½˝

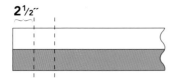

Cut 10 segments.

4. Arrange 2 segments from Step 3, as shown. Sew the segments together, carefully matching the center seam. Press. Make 5. Each unit should measure $4\frac{1}{2}'' \times 4\frac{1}{2}''$.

Make 5.

5. Arrange the 4 units from Step 1 and the 5 units from Step 4, taking care to position and turn them as shown.

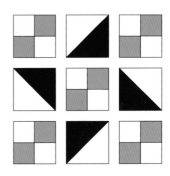

Sew the units together into rows. Press.

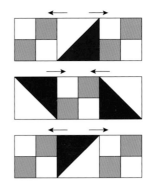

Sew the rows together, carefully matching the seams. Press. The block should measure $12\frac{1}{2}'' \times 12\frac{1}{2}''$.

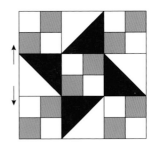

BLOCK 5

Spinning My Wheels

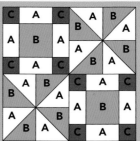

Cutting

Cut all strips from the crosswise grain of the fabric (from selvage to selvage).

FROM FABRIC A:

Cut 4 squares, $3\frac{7}{8}" \times 3\frac{7}{8}"$; cut each square once diagonally to make 2 half-square triangles (8 total).

Cut 1 strip, $2" \times 40"$; crosscut 8 pieces, $2" \times 3\frac{1}{2}"$.

FROM FABRIC B:

Cut 4 squares, $3\frac{7}{8}" \times 3\frac{7}{8}"$; cut each square once diagonally to make 2 half-square triangles (8 total).

Cut 2 squares, $3\frac{1}{2}" \times 3\frac{1}{2}"$.

FROM FABRIC C:

Cut 1 strip, $2" \times 40"$; crosscut 8 squares, $2" \times 2"$.

Assembling the Block

1. Sew a Fabric A half-square triangle and a Fabric B half-square triangle together. Press. Make 8. Each unit should measure $3\frac{1}{2}" \times 3\frac{1}{2}"$.

Make 8.

2. Arrange 4 units from Step 1, taking care to rotate them as shown.

Sew the units together into pairs. Press. Sew the pairs together, carefully matching the center seam. Press. Make 2. Each unit should measure $6\frac{1}{2}'' \times 6\frac{1}{2}''$.

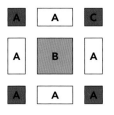

Make 2.

3. Arrange 4 Fabric C $2'' \times 2''$ squares, 4 Fabric A $2'' \times 3\frac{1}{2}''$ pieces, and a $3\frac{1}{2}'' \times 3\frac{1}{2}''$ Fabric B square.

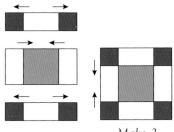

Sew the pieces and squares together into rows. Press. Sew the rows together, carefully matching the seams. Make 2. Each unit should measure $6\frac{1}{2}'' \times 6\frac{1}{2}''$.

Make 2.

4. Arrange the 2 units from Step 2 and the 2 units from Step 3.

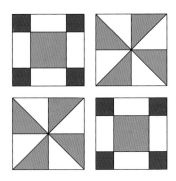

Sew the units together in pairs. Press.

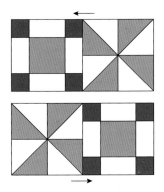

Sew the pairs together, carefully matching the center seam. Press.

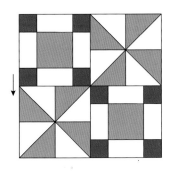

BLOCK 6

Useless Bay

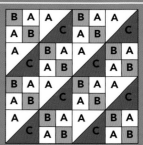

Cutting

Cut all strips from the crosswise grain of the fabric (from selvage to selvage).

FROM FABRIC A:
Cut 4 squares, $3^7/8'' \times 3^7/8''$; cut each square once diagonally to make 2 half-square triangles (8 total).

Cut 1 strip, $2'' \times 40''$.

FROM FABRIC B:
Cut 1 strip, $2'' \times 40''$.

FROM FABRIC C:
Cut 4 squares, $3^7/8'' \times 3^7/8''$; cut each square once diagonally to make 2 half-square triangles (8 total).

Assembling the Block

This block uses the Strip Piecing technique (page 20).

1. Sew a Fabric A half-square triangle and a Fabric C half-square triangle together. Press. Make 8. Each unit should measure $3^1/2'' \times 3^1/2''$.

Make 8.

2. Arrange the $2'' \times 40''$ Fabric A strip and the $2'' \times 40''$ Fabric B strip.

Sew the Fabric A strip and the Fabric B strip right sides together along a long edge. Press. The strip set should measure $3\frac{1}{2}'' \times 40''$.

3. Cut a total of 16 segments, each 2″ wide, from the strip set you made in Step 2.

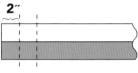

Cut 16 segments.

4. Arrange 2 segments from Step 3 as shown. Sew the segments together, carefully matching the center seam. Press. Make 8. Each unit should measure $3\frac{1}{2}'' \times 3\frac{1}{2}''$.

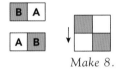

Make 8.

5. Arrange the 8 units from Step 1 and the 8 units from Step 4, taking care to position and turn them, as shown.

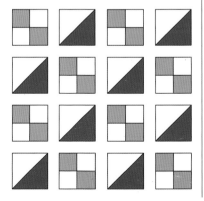

Sew the units together into rows. Press.

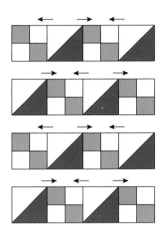

Sew the rows together, carefully matching the seams. Press. The block should measure $12\frac{1}{2}'' \times 12\frac{1}{2}''$.

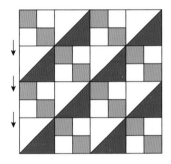

BLOCK 7

Jewel Box

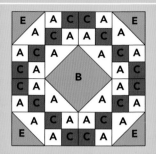

Cutting

Cut all strips from the crosswise grain of the fabric (from selvage to selvage).

FROM FABRIC A:

Cut 4 squares, $3\frac{1}{2}'' \times 3\frac{1}{2}''$.

Cut 2 squares, $3\frac{7}{8}'' \times 3\frac{7}{8}''$; cut each square once diagonally to make 2 half-square triangles (4 total).

Cut 1 strip, $2'' \times 40''$.

FROM FABRIC B:

Cut 1 square, $6\frac{1}{2}'' \times 6\frac{1}{2}''$.

FROM FABRIC C:

Cut 1 strip, $2'' \times 40''$.

FROM FABRIC E:

Cut 2 squares, $3\frac{7}{8}'' \times 3\frac{7}{8}''$; cut each square once diagonally to make 2 half-square triangles (4 total).

Assembling the Block

This block uses the Sew and Flip technique (page 21) and the Strip Piecing technique (page 20).

1. Use a ruler and marking tool to draw a diagonal line from corner to corner on the wrong side of each $3\frac{1}{2}'' \times 3\frac{1}{2}''$ Fabric A square. You will have 4 marked squares.

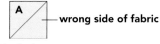

Mark 4 squares.

2. With right sides together and the corners aligned, place marked $3\frac{1}{2}'' \times 3\frac{1}{2}''$ Fabric A squares on opposite corners of the $6\frac{1}{2}'' \times 6\frac{1}{2}''$ Fabric B square. Sew directly on the diagonal lines.

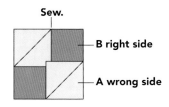

3. Cut away the excess fabric, leaving a $\frac{1}{4}''$ seam allowance. Press.

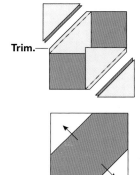

4. Repeat Steps 2 and 3 to sew a marked $3\frac{1}{2}'' \times 3\frac{1}{2}''$ Fabric A square to the remaining corners of the unit from Step 3. Trim and press. The unit should measure $6\frac{1}{2}'' \times 6\frac{1}{2}''$.

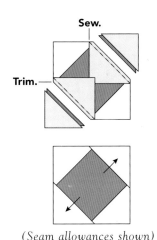

(Seam allowances shown)

5. Sew a Fabric A half-square triangle and a Fabric E half-square triangle together. Press. Make 4. Each unit should measure $3\frac{1}{2}'' \times 3\frac{1}{2}''$.

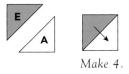

Make 4.

6. Arrange the $2'' \times 40''$ Fabric A strip and the $2'' \times 40''$ Fabric C strip as shown.

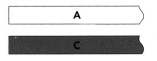

Sew the Fabric A strip and the Fabric C strip right sides together along one long edge. Press. The strip set should measure $3\frac{1}{2}'' \times 40''$.

7. Cut a total of 16 segments, each 2″ wide, from the strip set you made in Step 2.

Cut 16 segments.

8. Arrange 2 segments from Step 7 as shown. Sew the segments together, carefully matching the center seam. Press. Make 8. Each unit should measure $3\frac{1}{2}'' \times 3\frac{1}{2}''$.

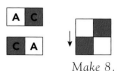

Make 8.

9. Arrange 2 units from Step 8, taking care to rotate them as shown. Sew the units together, carefully matching the seams. Press. Make 4. Each unit should measure $3\frac{1}{2}'' \times 6\frac{1}{2}''$.

Make 4.

10. Arrange the unit from Step 1, the 4 units from Step 5, and the 4 units from Step 9, taking care to position and turn them as shown.

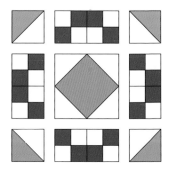

Sew the units together into rows. Press.

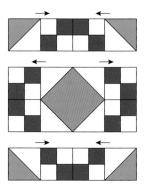

Sew the rows together, carefully matching the seams. Press. The block should measure $12\frac{1}{2}'' \times 12\frac{1}{2}''$.

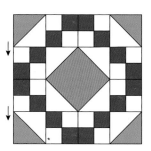

Tumbling Star

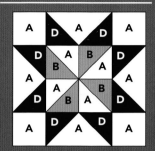

Cutting

Cut all strips from the crosswise grain of the fabric (from selvage to selvage).

 ### FROM FABRIC A:

Cut 2 squares, $3^7/8'' \times 3^7/8''$; cut each square once diagonally to make 2 half-square triangles (4 total).

Cut 4 rectangles, $3^1/2'' \times 6^1/2''$.   Cut 4 squares, $3^1/2'' \times 3^1/2''$.

 ### FROM FABRIC B:

Cut 2 squares, $3^7/8'' \times 3^7/8''$; cut each square once diagonally to make 2 half-square triangles (4 total).

 ### FROM FABRIC D:

Cut 8 squares, $3^1/2'' \times 3^1/2''$.

Assembling the Block

This block uses the Sew and Flip technique (page 21).

1. Sew a Fabric A half-square triangle and a Fabric B half-square triangle together. Press. Make 4. Each unit should measure $3^1/2'' \times 3^1/2''$.

Make 4.

2. Arrange the 4 units from Step 1, taking care to rotate them as shown.

Sew the units together into pairs. Press. Sew the pairs together, carefully matching the center seam. Press. The unit should measure $6^1/2'' \times 6^1/2''$.

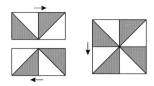

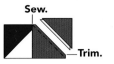

3. Use a ruler and marking tool to draw a diagonal line from corner to corner on the wrong side of each $3\frac{1}{2}'' \times 3\frac{1}{2}''$ Fabric D square. You will have 8 marked squares.

Mark 8 squares.

4. With right sides together and raw edges aligned, place a marked $3\frac{1}{2}''$ Fabric D square on one end of a $3\frac{1}{2}'' \times 6\frac{1}{2}''$ Fabric A rectangle, as shown. Sew directly on the diagonal line.

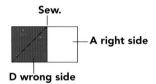

5. Cut away the excess fabric, leaving a $\frac{1}{4}''$ seam allowance. Press. Make 4.

Make 4.

6. Repeat Steps 4 and 5 to sew a marked $3\frac{1}{2}'' \times 3\frac{1}{2}''$ Fabric D square to the opposite end of the unit from Step 5. Trim and press. Make 4. Each unit should measure $3\frac{1}{2}'' \times 6\frac{1}{2}''$.

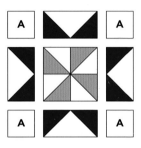

Make 4. (Seam allowances shown)

7. Arrange the unit from Step 2, the 4 units from Step 6, and the $3\frac{1}{2}'' \times 3\frac{1}{2}''$ Fabric A squares, as shown.

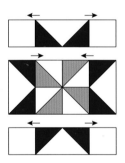

With right sides together and raw edges aligned, sew the units and squares into rows. Press.

Sew the rows together, carefully matching the seams. Press. The block should measure $12\frac{1}{2}'' \times 12\frac{1}{2}''$.

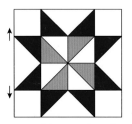

Ohio Star

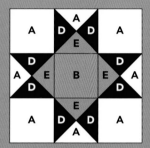

Cutting

Cut all strips from the crosswise grain of the fabric (from selvage to selvage).

FROM FABRIC A:

Cut 1 square, $5\frac{1}{4}'' \times 5\frac{1}{4}''$; cut twice diagonally to make 4 quarter-square triangles.

Cut 4 squares, $4\frac{1}{2}'' \times 4\frac{1}{2}''$.

FROM FABRIC B:

Cut 1 square, $4\frac{1}{2}'' \times 4\frac{1}{2}''$.

FROM FABRIC D:

Cut 2 squares, $5\frac{1}{4}'' \times 5\frac{1}{4}''$; cut each square twice diagonally to make 4 quarter-square triangles (8 total).

FROM FABRIC E:

Cut 1 square, $5\frac{1}{4}'' \times 5\frac{1}{4}''$; cut twice diagonally to make 4 quarter-square triangles.

Assembling the Block

1. Sew a Fabric A quarter-square triangle and a Fabric D quarter-square triangle together. Press. Make 4.

Make 4.

2. Repeat Step 1, using a Fabric D quarter-square triangle and a Fabric E quarter-square triangle. Press. Make 4.

Make 4.

3. Sew a unit from Step 1 and a unit from Step 2 together, carefully matching the center seam. Press. Make 4. Each unit should measure $4\frac{1}{2}'' \times 4\frac{1}{2}''$.

Make 4.

4. Arrange the 4 units from Step 3, the $4\frac{1}{2}'' \times 4\frac{1}{2}''$ Fabric A squares, and the $4\frac{1}{2}'' \times 4\frac{1}{2}''$ Fabric B square, taking care to turn the units as shown.

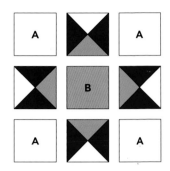

Sew the units and squares together into rows. Press.

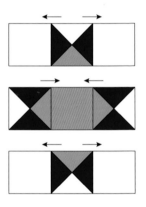

Sew the rows together, carefully matching the seams. Press. The block should measure $12\frac{1}{2}'' \times 12\frac{1}{2}''$.

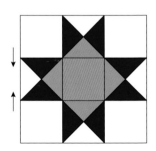

Assembling the Quilt

Once you've finished sewing the blocks, you are ready to put them together to complete the quilt top. This is an exciting time! You'll be sewing longer seams, so keep your pins handy and take care to maintain an accurate ¹⁄₄″ seam allowance.

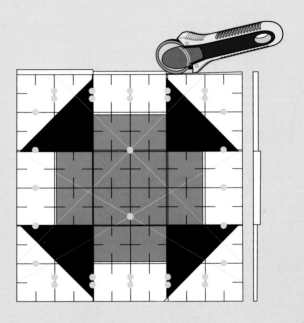

Squaring the Blocks

It's important that all your blocks are the same size in order for the pieces of the quilt top to fit together and for your finished quilt to be flat and square.

Measure each block. The unfinished measurement—that is, the measurement before the block is sewn into the quilt top—should be $12\frac{1}{2}'' \times 12\frac{1}{2}''$.

If your blocks vary slightly (less than ¹⁄₄″), you can probably use your rotary cutter and ruler to make the necessary adjustments. Trim the larger blocks to

match the smaller ones, taking care not to cut off any outside points (such as tips of the triangles in the Churn Dash block) and to maintain a ¹⁄₄″ seam allowance all around the outer edge of the block. To keep the block square, divide the excess measurement and remove an equal amount from all four sides, as shown.

If any of your blocks varies more than ¹⁄₄″ in size from the others, I suggest you remake that block. Before you begin, refer to the tip on page 18 to retest your ¹⁄₄″ seam for accuracy.

Sewing the Quilt Top

1. Arrange the Useless Bay, Tumbling Star, and Jewel Box blocks and 2 Fabric D $2\frac{1}{4}'' \times 12\frac{1}{2}''$ lattice strips, alternating them as shown. Sew the blocks and strips together to make Row 1. Press.

Repeat, using the Ohio Star, Spinning My Wheels, and Waterwheel blocks and 2 Fabric D lattice strips to make Row 2, and the Triple Rail, Churn Dash, and Log Cabin blocks and 2 Fabric D lattice strips to make Row 3.

2. Arrange 3 Fabric D $2\frac{1}{4}'' \times 12\frac{1}{2}''$ lattice strips and 2 Fabric E $2\frac{1}{4}'' \times 2\frac{1}{4}''$ squares, alternating them as shown. Sew the strips and squares together. Press. Make 2.

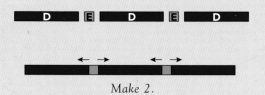

Make 2.

3. Arrange the rows from Step 1 and the units from Step 2, alternating them as shown. Sew the rows and units together. Press.

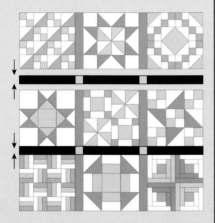

Adding Borders

This quilt is framed by two borders with squared corners. The first inner border is made from the same fabric as the lattice strips (Fabric D). The outer border is made from the Fabric B print.

Square borders are the easiest of all borders to sew. Add the top and bottom borders first. If the quilt top is slightly longer than the border, stitch with the quilt top on the bottom, closest to the feed dogs. If the reverse is true, stitch with the border on the bottom. The motion of the feed dogs will help ease in the extra length.

By measuring your pieced top before cutting your border lengths, you will minimize disparities in length.

Design Play!

Before deciding on the final layout of your quilt top, rearrange the blocks several times to make sure you have the design that best suits your taste. Be sure to maintain a pleasing visual balance and to limit the rows to three blocks each.

1. Sew the 5 Fabric D $2\frac{1}{4}'' \times 40''$ inner border strips together end to end to make one continuous strip.

2. Measure the finished quilt top through the center from side to side. Cut 2 inner borders to this measurement from the strip you made in Step 1. These will be the top and bottom inner borders.

3. Place pins at the center points of the top and bottom of the quilt top and at the center point of each border strip. Pin the borders to the quilt top, matching the ends and center points. Use additional pins as needed, easing or gently stretching the border to fit. Sew the borders to the quilt top with a $\frac{1}{4}''$ seam allowance. Press.

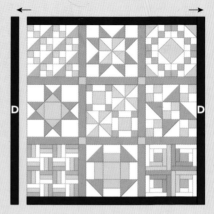

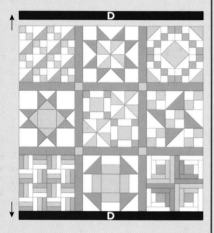

5. Sew the 5 Fabric B 6″ × 40″ outer border strips together end to end to make one continuous strip. Press.

6. Repeat Steps 2–4 to measure, cut, pin, and sew a Fabric B outer border strip to each side of the quilt. Press.

4. Measure the quilt from top to bottom, including the borders you've just sewn. Cut 2 borders to this measurement from the remaining long Fabric D strip. These will be the side inner borders. Repeat Step 3 to pin, sew, and press the borders.

Preparing Your Quilt for Quilting

Don't skimp in preparing your quilt for quilting! Take the time to layer it properly and baste it sufficiently. The result—a quilt free of puckers and bumps—will make you proud.

Carefully press the quilt top from the back to set the seams and then press from the front. If you wish, use spray starch or sizing. Use a pair of small scissors or snips to trim any stray threads that may shadow through to the front of the quilt.

Selecting and Marking Quilting Designs

Sources for quilting designs are everywhere. I recommend that you mark any quilting designs on your quilt top before you baste the layers together.

Quilting in the ditch (right beside the seamlines) and outline quilting (stitching $\frac{1}{4}''$ inside each shape) are two options that typically do not require marking.

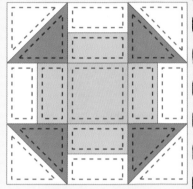

Outline quilting

You'll also want to explore the many choices available in quilting stencils and quilting pattern books, especially for the lattice strips and borders. Examine your fabrics; perhaps there is a motif or pattern you can outline or adapt for quilting.

Always test any marking tool (e.g., chalk, water-soluble marker, silver pencil) on scraps of your fabrics to be sure you can remove the marks easily after you've finished quilting.

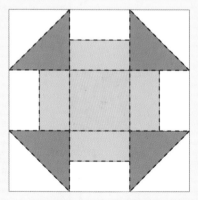

Quilting in the ditch

Choosing and Preparing Batting and Backing

The choice of batting is a personal decision, but you'll want to consider the method (and amount) of quilting you plan to do, as well as the quilt's end use. Because I prefer machine quilting, I usually use cotton batting in a heavier weight (any product identified as "extra" or "ultra" loft) for bed quilts and wallhangings. You'll probably want to stick with lightweight or low loft batting for hand quilting. Polyester batting is a good choice for tied quilts.

No matter which type of batting you choose, cut it approximately 4″ larger than the quilt top on all sides.

As with the batting, you'll want the quilt backing to be approximately 4″ larger than the quilt top on all sides. Unless you've selected an extra-wide fabric for the backing, you'll need to piece the fabric in order to have a large enough backing piece.

1. Prewash the backing fabric and remove the selvages.

2. Cut the 3½ yard piece of backing fabric in half across the width into 2 pieces, each approximately 40″ × 62½″. With right sides together, sew the pieces together along the 62½″ edges to make a backing piece approximately 80″ × 62½″. Press the seam open.

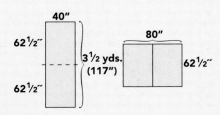

3. Trim the backing to $62\frac{1}{2}'' \times 62\frac{1}{2}''$. Set the leftover backing fabric aside. You may wish to use it for a hanging sleeve later (page 58)

Layering and Basting

I prefer to hand baste with thread for both hand and machine quilting.

1. Press the pieced backing fabric. Spread the backing wrong side up on a clean, flat surface and secure it with masking tape as shown. The fabric should be taut but not stretched.

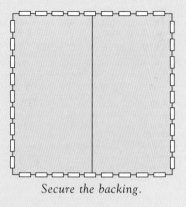

Secure the backing.

2. Center the batting over the backing. Center the quilt top right side up over the batting.

3. Thread a long needle with light-colored thread. Beginning in the center of the quilt, stitch a 4″ grid of horizontal and vertical lines.

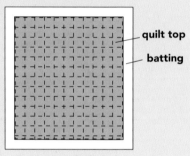

Basting with thread

4. When you've finished basting, remove the tape and get ready to quilt!

Quilting

A quilt becomes a quilt when it includes three layers—a top, a filler layer or batting, and a backing—all attached with stitching of some type to hold the layers together. (This means that to call your project a quilt, you need to finish it!) Some quilters create that stitching by hand; others, by machine.

Each step of the quiltmaking process, including the quilting, is exciting and fun to me. I love the idea of adding yet another level of creativity to my quilts.

Whether you quilt by hand or machine, the process will probably be new to you, so there is a learning curve involved. Practice is the best way to learn and master this skill. Here are some guidelines to get you started:

Machine Quilting

More and more quilters are turning to machine quilting to add that final layer of texture to their quilts. You'll need a special attachment or two for your sewing machine to machine quilt successfully.

Dual-Feed Foot

The dual-feed foot (also called a walking foot) is designed to hold and feed the three layers of your quilt evenly as you stitch. Use this foot to stitch single or parallel lines and grids—whether vertical, horizontal, or diagonal.

Use a dual-feed foot for straight-line quilting.

Start Quilting in the Middle

The very best place to begin your hand or machine quilting is right in the middle of your quilt. Starting in the center and working your way out to the borders helps keep the layers smooth and flat and avoids creating puckers and "hills" in the quilt surface, regardless of whether your quilting design uses straight or curved lines.

Open-Toe Stippling Foot

Also called a darning foot, the open-toe stippling foot allows you to quilt in all directions: you are the guide! Use this foot for following fabric motifs, quilting cables and other curved designs, meander quilting, and other free-motion techniques.

Use an open-toe foot for free-motion quilting.

You will need to drop the feed dogs on your sewing machine when you use the open-toe stippling foot. You might also need to set the presser foot pressure to the darning position so you can move the quilt at a smooth pace for consistent stitches. Some machines have a built-in stipple stitch, which is a wonderful way to achieve this beautiful surface texture.

Hand Quilting

There are many books on hand quilting. Check your local quilt store.

Finishing

The binding, hanging sleeve, and label of your quilt are important too, so be sure to give them the same attention you've given to every other element.

Squaring and Trimming the Quilt

Before adding the binding, you need to trim the excess batting and backing and square up your quilt. Use the seams of the outer borders as a guide.

1. Align a ruler with the outer-border seam and measure to the edge of the quilt in several places. Use the narrowest measurement as a guide for positioning your ruler and trim the excess batting, backing, and uneven border edge all around the quilt.

2. Fold the quilt in half lengthwise and crosswise to check that the corners are square and that the sides are equal in length. If they aren't, use a large square ruler to even them up, one corner at a time.

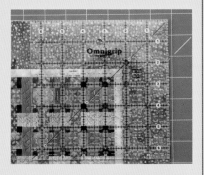

3. Stabilize the quilt edges by stitching around the perimeter with a basting or serpentine stitch. (Do not use a zigzag stitch, because it can push and pull the fabric out of shape.) If you have a dual-feed foot, this is a good time to use it!

4. Remove any stray threads or bits of batting from the quilt top. You are now ready to bind your quilt.

As a rule of thumb, cut
enough binding strips to go
around the perimeter (outside edges) of the quilt, plus
an extra 10″–12″ for seams,
corners, and the oops factor.

Making Double-Fold Straight-Grain Binding

Binding is an important and, sadly, often overlooked step in the quiltmaking process. Many a wonderful quilt is spoiled by a poorly sewn binding. Take your time and enjoy the process of stitching the binding to your quilt. You're coming down the home stretch now!

Typically, I cut binding strips 3″ wide from selvage to selvage across the width of the fabric. I make an exception and cut strips on the bias only when I want to create a special effect with a plaid or striped fabric or when I need to follow a curved or rounded edge.

1. Sew the 3″-wide Fabric B strips together at right angles, as shown. Trim the excess fabric from the seams, leaving a ¼″ seam allowance, and press the seams open.

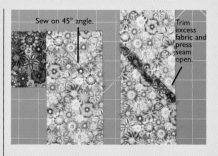

2. Fold the binding in half lengthwise, wrong sides together, and press.

Applying the Binding

The following method is the one I use to bind my quilts. It results in a finished edge that is attractive and strong.

1. Starting on the top edge, approximately 10″ from the upper left corner and with the raw edges even, place the binding on the quilt top. Check to see that none of the diagonal seams falls on a corner of the quilt. If one does, adjust the starting point. Begin stitching 4″ from the end of the binding, using a ½″ seam allowance.

2. Stitch about 2″ and then stop and cut the threads. Remove the quilt from the machine and fold the binding to the back of the quilt. The binding should cover the line of machine

stitching on the back. If the binding overlaps the stitching too much, try again, taking a slightly wider seam allowance. If the binding doesn't cover the original line of stitching, take a slightly narrower seam allowance. Remove the unwanted stitches before you continue.

3. Using the stitching position you determined in Step 2, resume stitching until you are $\frac{1}{2}$″ from the first corner of the quilt. Stop, backstitch, cut the thread, and remove the quilt from the machine.

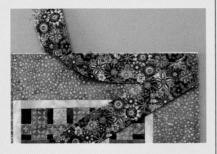

4. Fold the binding to create a mitered corner.

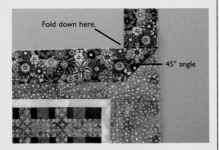

Fold down here.

45° angle

5. Resume stitching at edge of quilt, mitering each corner as you come to it.

6. Stop stitching about 3″ after you've turned the last corner. Make sure the starting and finishing ends of the binding overlap by at least 4″. Cut the threads and remove the quilt from the machine. Measure a 3″ overlap and trim the excess binding.

7. Place the quilt right side up. Unfold the unstitched binding tails, place them right sides together at right angles, and pin them together. Draw a line from the upper left corner to the lower right corner of the binding and stitch on the drawn line.

8. Carefully trim the seam allowance to $1/4"$ and press the seam open. Refold the binding and press. Finish stitching the binding to the quilt.

9. Turn the binding to the back of the quilt and pin it. (I pin approximately 12″ at a time.) Use matching-colored thread to blind-stitch the binding to the quilt back, carefully mitering the corners as you approach them. Hand stitch the miters on both sides.

Making and Adding a Sleeve

If you want to display your quilt on a wall, you need to add a sleeve to protect your work of art from excessive strain.

1. Cut an $8\frac{1}{2}"$-wide strip of hanging-sleeve fabric 1″ shorter than the width of the quilt. (If the quilt is wider than 40″, cut 2 strips and stitch them together end to end.) Fold under the short ends $1/4"$; stitch and press.

2. Fold the sleeve in half lengthwise, right sides together. Sew the long raw edges together and press the seam open. Turn the sleeve right side out and press again.

3. Mark the center points of the sleeve and the top edge of the quilt. Matching the center points, pin the sleeve to the quilt, right below the binding. Use matching-colored thread to blindstitch the top edge in place.

4. Push up the bottom edge of the sleeve a tiny bit so that when the hanging rod is inserted, it will not put strain on the quilt. Blindstitch the bottom edge of the sleeve, taking care not to catch the front of the quilt as you stitch.

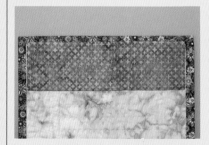

Making and Adding a Label

I always recommend making a label for your quilt. A label gives you a place to provide important information about both you and the quilt. I like to make my labels large—about 4″ × 7″—so I have plenty of room. You can sew the label to the lower right corner of the quilt back before it is quilted or wait to attach the label after you have completed the quilt.

I suggest including the following information on your label: the name of the quilt; your full name; your city, county, province or state, and country of residence; and the date.

If the quilt was made for a special person, to commemorate a special event, or as part of a series, you might want to include that information as well. You might also choose to note the name of the quilting teacher who inspired you or to tell a special story connected to the quilt.

Use the label to record key information about your quilt.

You can make a simple label by drawing and writing on fabric with permanent fabric markers. (Stabilize the fabric first with freezer paper or interfacing.) For a more elaborate (and fun!) label, try photo-transfer techniques, use the lettering system on your sewing machine, or use an embroidery machine to embellish your label. You could even create your own distinctive signature or logo. Include patches, decals, buttons, ribbons, or lace. I often include leftover blocks to tie the quilt top to the back.

Sampler Pillows

Made by M'Liss Rae Hawley, 2007

Finished pillow size: 16″ × 16″

Jewel Box

Ohio Star

Materials

All yardage is based on fabric that is 40″ wide after laundering. Amounts shown are for one pillow and do not include the center block.

¼ yard for the border

½ yard for the backing

16″ × 16″ pillow form

Cutting

Cut all strips across the fabric width. Cutting is for one pillow and does not include the center block. Refer to the appropriate block instructions for this information.

FROM THE BORDER FABRIC:
Cut 2 strips, 2½″ × 12½″.

Cut 2 strips, 2½″ × 16½″.

FROM THE BACKING FABRIC:
Cut 2 pieces, 16½″ × 10½″

Pillow Assembly

1. Choose and construct your favorite block from the 9 blocks shown in Making the Blocks (page 23).

2. Sew a $2\frac{1}{2}''$-wide border strip to the top and bottom of the block. Press. Repeat to sew $2\frac{1}{2}''$-wide borders to the sides. Press.

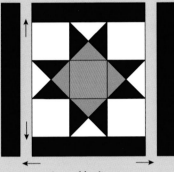

Assembly diagram

3. Fold under a $\frac{1}{4}''$ hem along one $16\frac{1}{2}''$ edge of each $16\frac{1}{2}'' \times 10\frac{1}{2}''$ backing piece. Press. Fold under another $\frac{1}{4}''$. Press and stitch along the folded edge.

4. With right sides up, place one backing piece over the other so the hemmed edges overlap, making the backing piece the same size as the pillow top. Baste the backing pieces together at the top and bottom where they overlap.

Quilting Your Pillow Top

If you wish, you can layer and quilt the pillow top before assembling it into a pillow. You'll need a 20″ × 20″ square each of batting—I used diaper flannel—and lining fabric. Refer to Preparing Your Quilt for Quilting (page 49) and Quilting (page 52) for guidance, as needed. Trim the batting and lining even with the pillow top after quilting.

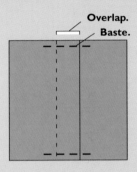

Overlap.
Baste.

5. With right sides together, align and pin the pillow top to the backing. Sew around the outside edges with a $\frac{1}{4}''$-wide seam. Remove the basting, trim the corners at an angle outside the stitched line (this reduces bulk in the corners), and turn the pillow cover right side out. Press before inserting the pillow form.

Four-Block Quilt

The completed quilt measures 37 ¾″ × 37 ¾″.

Materials

All yardage is based on fabric that is 40″ wide after laundering.
Amounts shown are for the entire quilt, including the four blocks.

FABRIC A | *(background fabric)* ¾ yards

FABRIC B | *(theme fabric for blocks, outer border, binding)* 1⅜ yards

FABRIC C | *(blocks)* ¼ yard

FABRIC D | *(blocks, lattice, inner border)* ⅞ yards

FABRIC E | *(blocks, cornerstones)* ⅛ yard

BACKING | 1⅜ yards *

BATTING | 41¾″ × 41¾″ *

* This small quilt adds only 2″ to all sides for backing and batting.

Cutting

Cut all strips across the fabric width.
Cutting is for quilt borders and does not
include the blocks. Refer to the appropriate
block instructions for this information.

FROM FABRIC B:

Cut 4 strips, 4½″ × 40″, for the
outer border.

Cut 4 strips, 3″ × 40″, for the binding.

FROM FABRIC D:

Cut 3 strips, 2¼″ × 40″, for the
inner border.

Cut 2 strips, 2¼″ × 40″;
crosscut 4 strips, 2¼″ × 12½″,
for the lattice.

FROM FABRIC E:

Cut 5 squares, 2¼″ × 2¼″,
for the lattice cornerstones.

Quilt Assembly

Follow the assembly instructions for
the individual blocks and general
quilt assembly instructions for adding
lattice, cornerstones, and borders.

Index

Other books by M'Liss

About the Author

M'Liss Rae Hawley is the best-selling author of nine books. She is an accomplished quilting teacher, lecturer, embroidery, and textile designer and conducts workshops and seminars worldwide. Although her new PBS television series, M'Liss's Quilting World, is in production, M'Liss still finds time to design fabric exclusively for Jo-Ann's stores, and to be the quilting spokesperson for Husqvarna Viking and Robison-Anton Textile Company. M'Liss and her husband, Michael, live on Whidbey Island, Washington, in a filbert orchard. Michael is also a best-selling author and recently retired as sheriff of Island County. Their son, Alexander, is a sergeant in the USMC, and their daughter, Adrienne, a recent college graduate of Seattle University, is serving in AmeriCorps. Michael and M'Liss share their home with seven dachshunds and four cats.